Who is Mary?

For Christians (followers of Jesus) Mary is the most important woman who ever lived because she agreed to become the Mother of God's only Son, Jesus. His birth, life, death, and rising from the dead changed our world forever. Jesus' words and actions continue to teach us how to love God, others, and ourselves so that someday we might be happy with God in heaven.

We know that Mary lived more than 2,000 years ago in a faraway town called Nazareth. Some people wrote stories about her life as a young Jewish girl and said her parents were Joachim and Ann. We can imagine that Mary played with friends and helped her family. She probably learned to make bread and spin threads from wool for cloth, helped her Mother mend clothing, and picked fruits and vegetables for their family meals.

To honor and remember Mary, the Catholic Church celebrates her birthday on September 8.

Questions: Why is Mary important to us? Why is Jesus important to us?

Activity: Find and color the foods Mary's family probably ate. (*Cucumbers, pomegranates, grapes, olives, and figs.*) Have you ever tasted these foods? Did you like them?

Mary Learns About God's Plan

Scripture (the Bible) says God sent an angel (a messenger) to ask Mary to become the Mother of God's only Son, Jesus. Angel Gabriel greeted Mary and called her "full of grace." That meant Mary was very special to God from the first moment of her life. For this reason, Mary is also special to us. Catholics go to church on December 8 to praise and thank God that Mary was and always will be "full of grace." This feast day is called *The Immaculate Conception.*

At first Mary was puzzled by what the Angel Gabriel said. Mary, however, loved God very much and said **yes** to God's plan. *(Cf. Lk 1:26-38)* Every year on March 25 Catholics remember and celebrate Mary's **yes** to God. This feast day is called *The Annunciation.*

To honor Mary, as the Mother of Jesus, the Catholic Church celebrates her Motherhood every year on January 1.

Questions: • What did God's messenger ask Mary?
• What did Mary say to the angel about God's question?

Activities: • Connect the dots to form the word Mary said to God. Then color this special word
• Tell about times when it is hard to say "yes" — telling the truth, picking up a mess you made, sharing a favorite treat or toy, obeying your parents.

Mary Helps Her Cousin Elizabeth

The Angel Gabriel told Mary that her older cousin Elizabeth would also have a Son. Mary was filled with God's love and wanted to share her joy and good news with her cousin. So Mary traveled to Elizabeth's home. She also wanted to show her love for God by helping Elizabeth and Zachary prepare for their new baby. Elizabeth, too, was filled with God's love and joy when Mary arrived. They both rejoiced and praised God together. Mary stayed with Elizabeth and Zachary for about three months, until the birth of Baby John. Then, she returned home. (Cf. Lk 1:5-23, 39-56)

Every year on May 31 Catholics celebrate Mary's visit to her cousin Elizabeth and remember Mary's wonderful prayer praising God. This feast day is called *The Visitation*.

Questions: • Who did Mary and Elizabeth praise for the good news about Jesus and John?
• How did Mary show her love for her relatives?

Mary's Prayer of Praise to God

I give praise and honor to you, O my God.

I am so happy because you are God our Savior.

From this day all people will call me blessed.

God, who is mighty, has done great things for me.

Holy is God's name. . . (Cf. Lk 1:47-49)

The prayer printed above is a simple version of a prayer called the *Magnificat*. The Bible tells us that Mary said this prayer at the home of her cousin after Elizabeth joyfully greeted her. Mary was so happy about the good news of Jesus' coming that she said this prayer to praise and thank God. Mary knew that God had blessed her and honored her by asking her to be the Mother of Jesus. (Cf. Lk 1:39-56)

God likes prayers that are joyful and prayers that include singing and dancing. God likes to see us happy.

Activity: Color and decorate the scroll.

Question: Why did Mary say the *Magnificat* prayer?

Mary and Joseph Travel to Bethlehem

It was God's plan that Mary would have a husband who would take care of her and help raise her Son. Like Mary, Joseph learned about God's plan from an angel. Like Mary, Joseph said **yes** to God. Joseph also said Mary's Son would be called "Jesus" as he had been told by the angel. (*Cf. Mt* 1:18-25)

While Mary and Joseph were waiting for Jesus to be born, the ruler over their country said everyone in the country had to be counted. So Mary and Joseph traveled to Bethlehem and put their names on the ruler's list. (*Cf. Lk* 2:1-6)

Activity: Draw a line to help Mary and Joseph find a path to Bethlehem.

Question: Why did Mary and Joseph travel to Bethlehem?

The Birth of Jesus

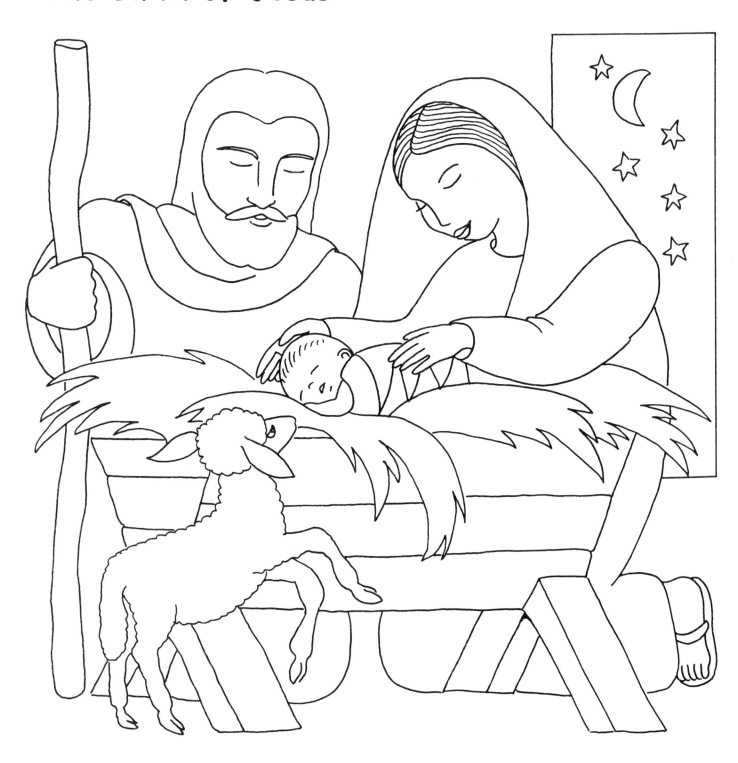

Bethlehem was very crowded with travelers when Mary and Joseph arrived. There was no room for them in the inn, so they stayed in a stable (a place to keep animals). While they were there, Jesus was born. Mary wrapped Baby Jesus in a blanket and gently laid him down in a manger (a feeding box for farm animals). (*Cf. Lk 2:6-7*) The promise made to Mary by God was fulfilled. She had given birth to God's only Son, Jesus.

Questions: • Whose birthday do we celebrate every year on Christmas Day, December 25?
           • What is a stable? What is a manger?

The Shepherds Visit Baby Jesus

In the fields not far from Bethlehem, there were some shepherds caring for their sheep. An angel appeared and told them the good news about Jesus' birth. Then more angels came. The shepherds heard them joyfully singing, "Glory to God in the highest and peace to God's people on Earth!" The shepherds were amazed by the angels. They hurried to Bethlehem. There they found Mary and Joseph with Baby Jesus lying in a manger. Then the shepherds hurried home and told the good news to others. They praised God for everything they had heard and seen that night. (Cf. Lk 2:8-20)

Activities: Add a moon and stars to the sky above the stable. Add a lamb next to the manger.

Question: What words did the shepherds hear the angels sing?

The Wise Men Visit Baby Jesus

Wise Men or Magi from faraway lands came to Bethlehem. A bright, shining star showed them the way to the newborn king. The Gospel of Matthew tells their story. The Wise Men were very happy when they found Jesus, Mary, and Joseph. After praising and giving Jesus gifts, they traveled back to where they lived. (Cf. Mt 2:1-17)

The visit of Wise Men from distant lands reminds us that Jesus came for all people and all nations. We remember the Wise Men's visit on *The Feast of the Epiphany*. This feast is celebrated on the second Sunday after Christmas.

Questions: • What helped the Wise Men find their way to Bethlehem?
• What did they do when they found Jesus, Mary, and Joseph?

Activity: Add the star that helped the Wise Men find Bethlehem.

Mary, Joseph, and Jesus Travel to Egypt

God's angel told Joseph in a dream that Jesus was in danger because King Herod wanted to harm him. The angel told Joseph to take his family to Egypt where they would be safe. Mary quickly packed and Joseph saddled their donkey. It was a long trip from Bethlehem to Egypt. Mary rode the donkey and held little Baby Jesus as Joseph led them on the dusty roads. It was a hard trip to make, but Mary and Joseph believed and trusted that God would guide and protect them. They stayed in Egypt until the king died. As promised, God's angel told Joseph in a dream that it was safe for them to return. So Joseph, Mary, and Jesus traveled back to make their home in Nazareth. (Cf Mt 2:13-23)

Activity: Draw and color the shortest path to follow from Bethlehem to Egypt.

Questions: • Why did Joseph, Mary, and Jesus travel to Egypt?
  • What items might Mary and Joseph have packed for their trip to Egypt?

Mary and Joseph Present Jesus in the Temple

Mary and Joseph wanted to obey all the laws of their Jewish faith. So they took Baby Jesus to the temple in Jerusalem. The temple was a very important place for prayer. There they thanked God for their new child and followed the custom of offering two young pigeons as a way of saying thank you. As a new Mother, Mary received a special blessing, too.

In the temple, two holy, elderly people saw Baby Jesus. One of them, Simeon, took Jesus in his arms and thankfully praised God. He told Mary and Joseph that Jesus would grow up to be a light to guide all people and that Jesus would bring great honor to the Jewish people. Simeon also told Mary she would have some very sad times, because not everyone would love her wonderful Son.

The other holy person in the temple was an elderly woman called Anna. Upon seeing Baby Jesus, she, too, praised and thanked God for Jesus' coming.

When they had finished the celebration at the temple, Jesus and his parents returned to their home in Nazareth. There Jesus lived happily with Mary and Joseph. He grew in strength and goodness and pleased God very much. (Cf. Lk 2:22-40)

Every year on February 2 Catholics celebrate *The Presentation*, when Mary and Joseph presented Baby Jesus in the temple. Candles are blessed and lit at church that day to remind us of Simeon's words that Jesus would be a light to guide all people.

Questions: • Why did Mary and Joseph take Jesus to the temple?
• What are the names of the two holy people in the temple?

Mary, Joseph, and Jesus in Nazareth

Jesus grew up with his parents in the small town of Nazareth. Mary and Joseph taught Jesus Jewish prayers and many other things as well. For example, Joseph taught Jesus his trade of carpentry (making things out of wood).

The Bible also tells us that Jesus grew and became strong, that he was very wise, and that God was very happy with him. (Cf. Lk 2:40) The Bible also says Jesus obeyed his parents, Mary and Joseph. (Cf. Lk 2:51)

Questions: • What type of work did Joseph do to support Mary and Jesus?
  • Do you obey your parent(s)?
  • In what ways do you help at home?

Mary and Joseph Find Jesus in the Temple

Every year Joseph, Mary, and Jesus traveled to Jerusalem to celebrate Jewish feasts like the Passover. The Passover celebrates God's rescue of the Jewish people from slavery in Egypt long before Jesus' birth. On their way home one year, when Jesus was twelve, Mary and Joseph suddenly realized that Jesus was not among the family members and friends who were walking with them. Mary and Joseph searched and searched and finally walked back to the city of Jerusalem. After three days of searching, Mary and Joseph were very surprised to find Jesus in the temple! They saw Jesus sitting among the teachers, listening to them and asking questions. Everyone was amazed at Jesus' understanding and his answers. When asked by Mary why he had left them, Jesus said, "Did you not know that I must be in my Father's house?" Mary and Joseph did not understand Jesus' answer. Then Jesus went back to Nazareth and was obedient to Mary and Joseph as he grew up; but Mary always remembered what had happened. (Cf. Lk 2:41-51)

Questions: • What Jewish feast day had Mary, Joseph, and Jesus celebrated in this story?
• How many days did Mary and Joseph search for Jesus?
• Where did Mary and Joseph find Jesus?
• What was Jesus doing in the temple?

Mary Asks Jesus' Help at the Wedding Feast

When Jesus began his ministry (work) of teaching people about God's love, he went with his Mother, Mary, to a wedding at Cana.

During the wedding celebration, those giving the party ran out of wine. Mary saw the problem and asked Jesus to help. Mary had complete trust in Jesus. Mary told the servants to do whatever Jesus asked them to do. Jesus told the servants, "Fill the six big jars with water from the well, draw some out, and take it to the man in charge." The servants did as they were told. The man tasted it and said to the bridegroom, "This is very good wine! You should have served this first." A miracle had happened! Jesus had changed the water into wine. (A miracle is something you can't explain that shows God's power and love.) Mary must have smiled. This was the first of many miracles Jesus did to help people believe that God loved them. (Cf. Jn 2:1-11)

Activity: Color every space in the jars that has a dot to discover Mary's message to you.

Questions: • Who asked Jesus to help?
• What does the word "miracle" mean?

Mary at the Cross with Jesus

Some people were not friends of Jesus. They were angry, saying: "He made himself God's Son." (*Jn* 19:7) They did not want to listen to Jesus' teachings. So they arranged with the Roman rulers to have Jesus suffer and die on a cross. Mary and Jesus' friend John were at the cross. Before Jesus died, he asked Mary to take care of John as her Son. And then Jesus asked John to take care of Mary as his Mother. After Jesus died, he was buried nearby in a new tomb. (*Cf Jn* 19:25-42)

Mary and Jesus' friends felt very sad. His friends thought Jesus would never come back, but as promised, "God raised him from the dead." (*Acts* 13:30) And that is why we celebrate the good news of Jesus' return on Easter and sing "Alleluia," which means "praise God!"

Questions: · Why did some people want Jesus to die on the cross?
· Who did Jesus ask to take care of his Mother?
· What does the word "Alleluia" mean?

Mary Prays with Jesus' Friends

During the weeks following Easter, the risen Jesus visited his mother, Mary, and his friends several times. Mary and other women often joined the apostles (special helpers of Jesus) in praying and praising God.

On the 50th day after Easter (called Pentecost) Jesus' helpers were suddenly filled with the Holy Spirit (God's love) and went out to begin sharing the good news about Jesus to all the people. (Cf *Acts* 1:12-14; 2:1-41) Pentecost is celebrated as the beginning or birthday of Jesus' Church.

Questions: • Who did Mary often pray with?
• What does the word "apostle" mean?
• What happened on Pentecost?

God Takes Mary To Heaven

At the end of Mary's life on Earth, God's love lifted Mary's body and spirit to heaven. She went to live with God and all the angels and saints.

As Catholics we believe Mary was especially blessed by God from the moment of her creation. Mary said **yes** to being the Mother of Jesus and to raising him with Joseph's help.

Heaven is the final home for those who love and obey God while on Earth, as Mary and Joseph did. God promises this and God keeps promises.

Mary's wonderful homecoming to heaven is remembered by the Catholic Church on August 15. This celebration day is called *The Assumption.*

Questions: • Where is Mary? (*With God in heaven.*)
  • Can we see Mary, God or Heaven? (*No, not now, but someday we hope to see and be with them in heaven, too.*)

Activity: Draw faces on the people who are in heaven.

Mary's Importance to Us

reminds us that Mary is the **Mother** of God's only Son, Jesus, who came to show us how much God loves and cares for us.

reminds us that our loving **A**ctions show people we are followers of Jesus.

reminds us to **R**espect others (*show love in words and deeds*), as Jesus asks us to do.

reminds us that we should be like Mary and say **Y**es to God in our life. We learn about God's plan by:
- listening to our parents and teachers;
- studying and learning in school;
- singing and praising God in church;
- listening to God speak to us quietly in our heart.

Activity: Color the letters and flowers.

Titles Honoring Mary

Our Lady of Guadalupe

    In 1531, Mary was seen by a poor, older Mexican man named Juan Diego. Mary told Juan to ask his bishop to build a church on the hill where she appeared. Juan's bishop asked Juan for a sign from Mary. Juan went back to the place where he had first seen Mary and found roses growing there even though roses don't grow in winter. Mary picked some of the roses and put them inside Juan's cloak. Juan went to show his bishop the roses. When he opened his cloak, the flowers fell out and a beautiful colored picture of Mary was painted on his cloak. The church was built in Mexico and millions of visitors have come to pray at the church ever since. We remember and celebrate this story each year on December 12. It is called the feast of *Our Lady of Guadalupe*.

Questions: • What was the name of the man who saw Mary?
               • What did Mary ask the man to do?

Titles Honoring Mary

Our Lady of Lourdes

The year was 1858 and Bernadette was 14. In a cave near a river in Lourdes, France, Bernadette saw Mary eighteen times. Bernadette said Mary was beautiful and always smiled at her. She was dressed in white and wore a blue sash. Mary had messages from her Son, Jesus. "Pray for sinners," Mary said, "and pray that sick people will be healed." She instructed Bernadette to dig a little hole under a certain rock in the cave. Later that day, a spring began to flow from that spot down into the river.

Soon, sick people said they got well after bathing in the spring water. Mary's visits and the reports of sick people who got well bathing in the spring began to attract many visitors. Four years later a chapel was built at the cave. Then much later, in 1901, a huge church was finished. Many visitors travel every year to Lourdes to remember Mary, to pray, and to worship God.

Bernadette grew up and became a sister. She died in 1879 after a long illness. Years later, the Catholic Church named Bernadette a saint. (A saint is a person who is with God in heaven). She earned the title of saint for her life of praying and obeying God.

The Catholic Church remembers and celebrates Mary's visits to Lourdes on February. 11.

Questions: • Why do people want to visit Lourdes?
- What is a saint?

Titles Honoring Mary

Our Lady of Fatima / Our Lady of the Rosary

In 1917, Mary came to visit three poor children at Fatima in the country of Portugal. There was a terrible war in nearby countries. Mary's message to the children was to pray that the war would end and to pray the rosary for peace. Mary showed the children — Jacinta, Francisco, and Lucia — how to say the rosary. On Mary's last visit, many people saw the sun spinning in bright colors. It looked as if the sun would fall. After seeing this, many people believed that the three children had seen Mary. Also on her last visit to the children, Mary called herself *Our Lady of the Rosary.*

After these events Fatima became a very popular place for prayer. A large church was built near the place where Mary visited the three children. Two of the children, Jacinta and Francisco, died soon after Mary's visits. Lucia, however, grew up and became a sister. We remember Mary's visits and celebrate her title as *Our Lady of the Rosary* on October 7.

Activity: With the help of your family or teacher, say the rosary. (The four prayers used to say the rosary are provided on the next four pages.)

Prayers of the Rosary

The Apostles' Creed

I believe in God, the Father Almighty, creator of heaven and earth.
(I believe in God, who created heaven and earth.)

I believe in Jesus Christ, his only Son, our Lord.
(I believe in Jesus Christ, God's only Son.)

**He was conceived by the power of the Holy Spirit
and born of the Virgin Mary.**
(I believe that through the power of the Holy Spirit, Jesus was born of the Virgin Mary.)

He suffered under Pontius Pilate, was crucified, died, and was buried.
(I believe Jesus lived, suffered, died on a cross, and was buried.)

He descended to the dead. On the third day He arose again.
(I believe Jesus rose from the dead and came back to life. We celebrate this on Easter.)

He ascended into heaven, and is seated at the right hand of the Father.
(I believe Jesus returned to God, his Father, in heaven.)

He will come again to judge the living and the dead.
(I believe Jesus will come back someday to judge all people.)

I believe in the Holy Spirit,
(I believe in the Holy Spirit, whom Jesus sent to be with us.)

the holy catholic Church,
(I believe in the holy catholic Church.)

the communion of saints,
(I believe in God's family of believers, both living and dead.)

the forgiveness of sins,
(I believe God forgives sins.)

the resurrection of the body, and life everlasting.
(I believe that after we die, God will bring us back to a new life.)

Amen.
(Yes, I agree, I believe!)

The first prayer said in saying the rosary is the *Apostles' Creed*. This prayer lists twelve key beliefs of our Christian Faith. The word "apostle" means a special helper of Jesus. Jesus chose twelve apostles and sent them to tell people about his life, his teachings, and his love for them.

Activities: • Read and talk about each of the twelve beliefs with your teacher or parent(s).
  • Add decorations around this prayer.

Prayers of the Rosary

Glory and Praise To God

Father

**Glory be
to the Father,**
(Praise be to God the Father.)

and to the Son,
(Praise be to God's Son, Jesus.)

and to the Holy Spirit.
(Praise be to God the Holy Spirit.)

As it was in the beginning,
(Praise be to God yesterday.)

is now, and ever shall be,
(Praise be to God today.)

world without end. Amen.
(Praise be to God tomorrow.)

Spirit

Son

This prayer of praise refers to **one God** in three persons — the Father, the Son (Jesus), and the Holy Spirit. This mystery (something we can't fully understand) of one God who is Father, Son, and Holy Spirit is called the **Trinity.**

The Hand, Cross, and Dove in a triangle are signs often used in Christian art to represent God the Father, the Son (Jesus), and the Holy Spirit.

Activities: • Practice saying this prayer.
              • Connect the lines to form a solid triangle.

Prayers of the Rosary

The Hail Mary

Hail Mary, full of grace,
(*Greetings, Mary! God lives in your heart.*)

the Lord is with you. Blessed are you among women
(*You are God's special friend, and a very special woman.*)

and blessed is the fruit of your womb, Jesus.
(*You are the Mother of Jesus.*)

Holy Mary, Mother of God,
(*Mary, you are so good. You are the Mother of God's Son, Jesus.*)

Pray for us sinners,
(*Please, ask God to help us be good.*)

Now and at the hour of death. Amen.
(*Be with us always. Be with us when we're happy,
and when we're sad or afraid. Amen.*)

The *Hail Mary* is a very popular prayer taken from two Bible stories. The first is the story of Angel Gabriel's greeting to Mary when he told her God wanted her to be the Mother of His only Son, Jesus. (*Cf. Lk* 1:28) [See pg. 2.] The second is the wonderful greeting Mary received from her cousin Elizabeth. Mary went to visit and help her cousin after learning from the angel that Elizabeth was going to have a son, too. (*Cf. Lk* 1:42) [See pg. 3.]

Activities: • With the help of your teacher or parent(s) practice saying the *Hail Mary.*
• Color the picture of Mary and the Angel Gabriel.

Prayers of the Rosary

The *Our Father*

The prayer Jesus taught us.

Our Father, who art in heaven,
hallowed be thy name.
(*God is very special. We praise God!*)

Thy kingdom come;
thy will be done on earth as it is in heaven.
(*We should obey God's laws.*)

Give us this day our daily bread;
(*We ask God to give us what we need.*)

and forgive us our trespasses
as we forgive those who trespass against us;
(*God forgives us when we are sorry.
We should forgive others, too.*)

and lead us not into temptation,
but deliver us from evil. Amen.
(*We ask God to help us to be good and to protect us.*)

(Cf. *Mt* 6:9-13)

Jesus prayed often — sometimes alone and sometimes with friends. Jesus wants us to pray and gave us a special prayer to teach us how to pray. This prayer is called the *Lord's Prayer* or *Our Father*. It is said by Christians (friends of Jesus) all over the world.

Activities: • With the help of your teacher and/or parent(s) practice saying the *Our Father*.
• Color the flowers around the prayer that Jesus gave to us all.